Did you know? CHELMSFORD

A MISCELLANY

Compiled by Julia Skinner

With particular reference to the work of Russell Thompson

THE FRANCIS FRITH COLLECTION

www.francisfrith.com

First published in the United Kingdom in 2011 by The Francis Frith Collection®

This edition published exclusively for Identity Books in 2011 ISBN 978-1-84589-575-4

Text and Design copyright The Francis Frith Collection®
Photographs copyright The Francis Frith Collection® except where indicated.

The Frith® photographs and the Frith® logo are reproduced under licence from
Heritage Photographic Resources Ltd, the owners of the Frith® archive and trademarks.
'The Francis Frith Collection', 'Francis Frith' and 'Frith' are registered trademarks of
Heritage Photographic Resources Ltd.

All rights reserved. No photograph in this publication may be sold to a third party other than in the original
form of this publication, or framed for sale to a third party. No parts of this publication may be reproduced,
stored in a retrieval system, or transmitted, in any form, or by any means, electronic, mechanical, photocopying,
recording or otherwise, without the prior permission of the publishers and copyright holder.

British Library Cataloguing in Publication Data

Did You Know? Chelmsford - A Miscellany
Compiled by Julia Skinner
With particular reference to the work of Russell Thompson

The Francis Frith Collection
Oakley Business Park,
Wylye Road, Dinton,
Wiltshire SP3 5EU
Tel: +44 (0) 1722 716 376
Email: info@francisfrith.co.uk
www.francisfrith.com

Printed and bound in Malaysia

Front Cover: **CHELMSFORD, HIGH STREET 1919** 69010p
Frontispiece: **CHELMSFORD, TINDAL STREET 1919** 69014

The colour-tinting is for illustrative purposes only, and is not intended to be historically accurate

AS WITH ANY HISTORICAL DATABASE, THE FRANCIS FRITH ARCHIVE IS CONSTANTLY BEING
CORRECTED AND IMPROVED, AND THE PUBLISHERS WOULD WELCOME INFORMATION ON
OMISSIONS OR INACCURACIES

CONTENTS

- 2 Introduction
- 4 Essex Dialect Words and Phrases
- 5 Haunted Chelmsford
- 6 Chelmsford Miscellany
- 46 Sporting Chelmsford
- 48 Quiz Questions
- 50 Recipes
- 52 Quiz Answers
- 54 Francis Frith - Pioneer Victorian Photographer

INTRODUCTION

Two rivers, the Can and the Chelmer, come together at Chelmsford. The Can takes its name from the village of Great Canfield, where it rises. It is little more than a trickle above the town, but its flow is greatly boosted at Lawford Lane by the incoming waters of the River Wid. In fact, it used to be known in Chelmsford as the Great River. The Chelmer has its source at Wimbush in north-west Essex. Contrary to popular etymology, it takes its name from Chelmsford, rather than vice versa. For a long time it was simply called the Chelmsford River, and it is possible that, below the town, its early name was the Baddow. Having united with the Can, the Chelmer flows east towards its tidal estuary at Maldon, where it is joined by the River Blackwater.

People were living alongside the River Chelmer, one mile east of the present town, by around 2,500BC. They left traces of a long, straight earthen enclosure called a cursus; the function of this prehistoric monument is a mystery, but the cursus was surrounded by a number of small burial mounds and was probably used for ceremonial or ritual purposes. The site of the earthwork has now disappeared under the car park of the Asda supermarket in Chelmer Village. By the late Bronze Age (c900 BC) there was another settlement at Springfield Lyons, which included a sword factory as well as dwellings – we know this from the vast cache of sword-shaped clay moulds that was found during excavation of the enclosure ditch on the site. Some roundhouses from the later Iron Age period stood where the Parkway car park now is. However, it was not until the Roman invasion of Britain in the first century AD that anything approaching a town was established here, when a Roman military post was set up at the point where the Roman road from London to Colchester bridged the River Can. After a while, this developed into a small town called 'Caesaromagus', meaning either 'Caesar's market place' or 'Caesar's plain' – the only town in Britain to bear Caesar's name.

Did You Know?
CHELMSFORD
A MISCELLANY

The Roman administration of Britain ended in the early fifth century. The Roman town of 'Caesaromagus' was abandoned, and everything had crumbled away by the time the Saxons arrived in the Dark Ages – even the bridge over the Can. The new settlers avoided the old, low-lying site, preferring to live on higher ground near what is now Rectory Lane. Nevertheless, one particular East Saxon – a man called Ceolmaer – was in some way connected with a ford across the smaller of the two local rivers, and gave his name to it: Ceolmaer's ford, which became 'Chelmsford', although there was no town there at that time.

By the time of the Norman Conquest of 1066, the main area of settlement in the Chelmsford area was the Upland, a spur of high ground north of the present town centre. The local peasants worked as bonded labourers at a farm near the top of New Street. This was known as Bishop's Hall, because successive Bishops of London had owned it since the reign of Edward the Confessor (1042-1066). It remained in episcopal hands until 1545, when Bishop Bonner presented it to the Crown. Around the year 1100, a bridge was built over the Can by Bishop Maurice of London. The new bridge was built on the line of the old Roman road through 'Caesaromagus', but there was still no town there yet.

Chelmsford as we now know it was founded in 1199 by William de Sainte-Mère-Église, Bishop of London, when King John granted him the right to hold a market once a week, on Fridays, on a lane that is now the High Street. He divided the land on either side of the lane into plots that people could purchase as freeholds. Situated on the main road from London to Colchester, Chelmsford was ideally placed for such an enterprise. In time, a triangular market place appeared, the market-stalls became permanent shops, and a church was built to serve the new community. Chelmsford thrived as a busy market town, its central position meant it was a convenient place for Essex's assizes to be held, and by the mid 13th century it had become the county town, which it still remains.

ESSEX DIALECT WORDS AND PHRASES

'Bald' - white-faced animals, as in pub names such as **'The Baldfaced Stag'.**

'Barmed' - dirtied with mud.

'Clung' - lumps of wet mud or freshly dug earth.

'Dew' - if (but also used for 'if not').

'Dodman' - a name for a snail, and thus used for a lazy person or animal.

'Gant', or **'gantway'** - an alleyway between houses.

'Pollywags' - tadpoles.

'Rooning' - gathering mushrooms.

'Slud' - sludgy mud.

'Sobbled' - soaked, as in wet clothes.

'Venturemous' - bold, brave.

'Twitchell' - an alleyway.

'Tye' - a village green, as in the placename of Matching Tye.

'The hammer of it' - the long and the short of it.

HAUNTED CHELMSFORD

The building on the southern corner of Waterloo Lane in Chelmsford – Bank Chambers – was built in the 1890s on the site of the White Horse Inn. It is allegedly haunted by the ghost of Thomas Kidderminster, an Ely farmer who was murdered by the innkeeper in 1654. His body was buried in the inn yard and was not discovered for several years.

The Spotted Dog pub which used to stand in Tindal Street (see photograph 69016 on page 43) was also said to be haunted: it had a sealed room that emitted 'strange tappings'.

The early 18th-century house known as Springfield Place at Springfield (see photo below) that stands to the east of the church, overlooking the village green, was once the home of John Strutt, who owned the mills at Moulsham and Springfield. A more unseemly occupant is 'the squat figure of a man', who has haunted the building at various points in its history: the last sighting was in the 1940s, when Hoffmann's (the ball-bearing firm in Chelmsford) were using The Place as a hostel for their workers.

SPRINGFIELD, THE PLACE 1906 56905

CHELMSFORD MISCELLANY

Chelmsford's High Street used to be much wider than it is now. In the town's early years some of the freeholders had been setting up market stalls in the middle of the road, and by the end of the 14th century these became permanent structures, a block of shops called Middle Row which is still in situ today. These buildings split the road into what we now call High Street and Tindal Street, although their original names were Fore Street and Back Street. The level area where the market place opened out was called Cornhill. Here, in the middle of all the people, animals and carts, stood the Market Cross – an open-sided structure consisting of a roof supported on wooden posts. Just behind it, backing onto the edge of the churchyard, was the Tollhouse, an administrative office where the market tolls were collected, and where the manor-court sat. Chelmsford was an assize town, and the court hearings were sometimes held in the Tollhouse, sometimes in the Market Cross.

Essex people played a significant part in the Peasants' Revolt of 1381, and undoubtedly Chelmsford people were involved. According to information in the village church of St Mary of Great Baddow, a picturesque village that is now part of Chelmsford, the 'Men of Essex' gathered near the church with their leader, Jack Straw, from where they marched to London. The rebels rallied at Mile End on the outskirts of London, only to see their figurehead, Wat Tyler, killed in a scuffle. On 14 June 1381 the 14-year-old king, Richard II, pacified the rebels by giving each man a charter promising to honour their demands. However, on 1st July King Richard and his officials arrived in Chelmsford where they stayed for six days (probably lodging in the royal palace at Writtle), during which time they issued letters quashing the charters that the rebels had received, and tried local rebels. About 30 local men were hanged on the gallows on what is now Primrose Hill for their part in the uprising. Also executed in Chelmsford was Thomas Baker, a landowner from Fobbing who was one of the instigators of the revolt.

Did You Know?
CHELMSFORD
A MISCELLANY

Of interest in photograph 69011 (below) are the two (separate) shops on the right hand side of the High Street: Bolingbroke & Sons (nearest the camera) and its neighbour, Wenley Ltd. The former dealt in drapery, and the latter sold carpets, wallpaper and timber. They traded next door to each other for decades before merging in 1967. In 1921, Bolingbroke's had Chelmsford's first-ever in-store Santa at Christmas time, and two years later Wenley's was the first Chelmsford store to install a lift. The two neighbouring stores merged in 1967 and became one of Chelmsford's great institutions, particularly famed for their top-floor restaurant. They finally left the High Street in 2000.

CHELMSFORD, HIGH STREET 1919 69011

Did You Know?
CHELMSFORD
A MISCELLANY

Moulsham – 'Mul's Farm' – is the name for the part of Chelmsford lying south of the River Can, but in earlier times it was a settlement in separate ownership – until the 16th century it belonged to the Abbot of Westminster in London, whilst the Upland manor belonged to the Bishop of London. Chelmsford's buildings met Moulsham's at the bridge over the Can. The present bridge (known variously as Stone Bridge, Moulsham Bridge or Bishop's Bridge), seen in photograph C73043, opposite, was built by John Johnson, the County Surveyor, in the 1780s. It replaced a three-arched 14th-century bridge that was built by Henry Yevele, the king's master mason.

CHELMSFORD, MOULSHAM STREET 1919 69019

Did You Know?
CHELMSFORD
A MISCELLANY

CHELMSFORD, THE STONE BRIDGE c1955 C73043

St John's Church in Moulsham Street was built in 1837. Moulsham had never had its own church before this date, having been simply a hamlet in the parish of Chelmsford, and Moulsham people therefore had to use Chelmsford's church. This caused problems during an outbreak of plague in the 17th century, when Chelmsford's parish officers placed armed guards on the bridge across the Can 'to keepe Mousam from coming to bury there infected dead in ye churchyard'. They had good reason to take precautions – the plague did, indeed, begin in Moulsham before spreading to Chelmsford.

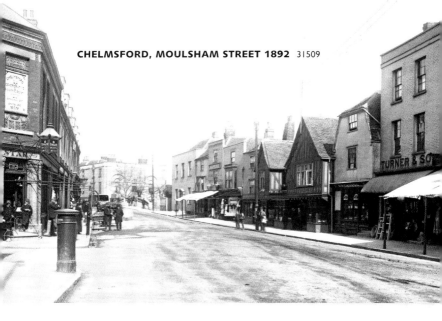

CHELMSFORD, MOULSHAM STREET 1892 31509

The Foster's shop with the blind seen on the left of photograph C73043 on page 9 stood on the site of Chelmsford's first gaol. In 1666 Chelmsford acquired the County Gaol in place of Colchester, and the Cross Keys pub on the south-west corner of the old medieval bridge over the Can was converted into a gaol. A pub on the opposite side of the road adopted the 'Cross Keys' name instead – the half-timbered pub seen on the right of photograph 31509, above, which was dismantled in 1912 to make way for the Regent Theatre, later the Regal Cinema (the site is now Chicago's). The old gaol was refashioned in 1777, but a new County Gaol was built at the top of Springfield Hill in the 19th century, and the old gaol was demolished in 1859. The old prison site was used as a parade ground by the West Essex Militia, hence the current street name of Barrack Square. The square building in the centre background of the above view (31509) was the Old Cock Inn, which was replaced by the Wesleyan church in 1898, as seen in the centre background of photograph 69018 on the opposite page.

Did You Know?
CHELMSFORD
A MISCELLANY

This shows almost the same view as the 1890s' photograph 31509 on the previous page, in 1919. By this date, the Cross Keys seen in the earlier photograph has been replaced by the Regent Theatre. The octagonal tower seen in the distance is that of the Wesleyan Church, which had replaced the Old Cock Inn. Built in 1898, the Wesleyan Church had seating for 800 people, and a commodious schoolroom at the back. The latter was linked to the main building by a bridge across the Gullet – a small channel connecting the Rivers Chelmer and Can. The Wesleyan church was demolished in the 1960s and replaced by the skyscraping Cater House; it is also shown in the background of photograph 41503 on page 15.

CHELMSFORD, MOULSHAM STREET 1919 69018

The figure in the photograph on the opposite page, at the corner of Baddow Road and Moulsham Street outside Loveday's Jewellers, is part of a sculpture called 'Guardian Figures' that was unveiled in 1999. On one side is a depiction of a Roman centurion, recalling Chelmsford's Roman origins. On the other is a Dominican friar, recalling the Dominican priory that was established in the mid 13th century at the north end of Moulsham, in the area now known as Friar's Walk. The priory was closed in the 16th century, as part of Henry VIII's Dissolution of the Monasteries. After the Dissolution, amongst other things, the vacated priory building was an early home of the King Edward VI Grammar School, which in 1551 was housed in the friars' former refectory (dining room). The late 15th-century timber-framed buildings on the right of photograph 69020 (below) of Moulsham Street were known as The Friars, having once abutted onto the gatehouse of the priory. The priory buildings had steadily collapsed after the Dissolution, and these last remnants were demolished in 1931 and replaced by a block of modern shops – which was in turn swept away by the development of Parkway in 1967.

CHELMSFORD, MOULSHAM STREET 1919 69020

Did You Know?
CHELMSFORD
A MISCELLANY

**CHELMSFORD
ROMAN CENTURION
2005** C73702

CHELMSFORD
A MISCELLANY

The Dominican friars at Chelmsford's priory did not just exist in a spiritual bubble – they were civil engineers too. In 1341 they provided themselves with water by linking their house to a spring, the Burgess Well, on the other side of the Can. This was achieved with a series of underground pipes and culverts. The well – which took its name from John Burgeys, a 13th-century landowner – now lies beneath the Fairfield Road car park. Its importance in Chelmsford's story cannot be overstated – it contributed to the town's water supply until 1973. It may also have been the friars who installed the elm pipes that channelled some of the Burgess Well's water to a conduit in the market place at the top of the High Street. Emerging from this conduit, the water flowed down the road as an open stream, before turning left into Springfield Road. It finally disgorged itself into the Gullet – a man-made backwater that linked the town's two rivers. In the centre of photograph 41503 on the opposite page, top, is the elegant stone rotunda that was erected in 1814 in the market place to mark the conduit head. The new conduit head became a long-term feature of the town. Within a few years, the market place was being called Conduit Square, and Back Street had become Conduit Street (these names were later changed to Tindal Square and Tindal Street). In 1851 the members of Chelmsford's Board of Health shut off the conduit stream, and replaced the domed conduit-head rotunda with Judge Tindal's statue (see page 31). From then on, Conduit Square became known as Tindal Square, and Back Street, or Conduit Street, had become Tindal Street. In 1852 the rotunda was moved to the position seen in this view, standing at the junction of Springfield Road and High Street. In 1939 the conduit head rotunda was moved again, to its present location in Tower Gardens which adjoin Admiral's Park, as seen in photograph C73032 on the opposite page, below. Tower Gardens took their name from a water tower that formerly stood there, so this is a nice continuation of the watery connection with the gardens!

CHELMSFORD, HIGH STREET 1898 41503

CHELMSFORD, TOWER GARDENS c1955 C73032

Someone who came to Chelmsford to make his fortune in the early 16th century was Thomas Mildmay, who set up a cloth stall in the market in 1506. He evidently did well, for by 1524 he was the second richest man in Chelmsford. Three of his five sons followed their father's trade, but the other two went into government service. Since breaking free from the Church of Rome, Henry VIII had been busy dissolving monasteries and generally appropriating Church property. The clothier's eldest son, another Thomas Mildmay, was employed as a royal auditor in assessing the value of these ill-gotten gains. Among the king's new acquisitions was Chelmsford's Dominican priory. By the time the royal assessors came knocking there were only seven brothers living there. They were given a little money and turfed out, after which Thomas Mildmay the younger bought the priory from the Crown. Westminster Abbey also had to surrender the manor of Moulsham to the Crown and in 1563 Thomas Mildmay bought that too, from Queen Elizabeth I, making this the first time that the manors of both Chelmsford and Moulsham had shared the same owner.

Under the abbots of Westminster, the manor of Moulsham had centred on a farmhouse lying in the fields south-west of Mousham Street. Thomas Mildmay demolished the farmhouse and had it rebuilt. He called it Moulsham Hall, and he and his successors chose to live there rather than at Bishop's Hall, which they leased out. Moulsham Hall stood roughly at the entrance to Moulsham County Junior and Infants Schools. Various members of the family modernized, extended or rebuilt it between the 16th and 18th centuries, most notably Benjamin Mildmay who turned it into an imposing classical-style edifice, all pilasters and pediments – this work was completed in 1743. In 1809, however, Moulsham Hall had become ruinous and had to be pulled down, and all traces are now gone.

Thomas Mildmay, the royal auditor, died in 1566 – the photograph below shows him as he is depicted in his tomb in Chelmsford Cathedral. In the terms of his will he left instructions that his estate – which now consisted of both Moulsham and Chelmsford – should remain in one piece as it passed to his successive male heirs. This bequest was known as the Mildmay Entail, and the constraints of this were to restrict the town's expansion until the early decades of the 19th century (see page 33).

There used to be a leper hospital in Mousham Street in the Middle Ages. When leprosy faded away, other types of invalids were cared for there. By the 1570s, the hospital was being referred to as 'the poor house'. One of the Mildmays pulled the hospital down in 1616 and built a row of six almshouses on the site. They were later remodeled by another member of the Mildmay family, and are still there today.

**CHELMSFORD
THE CATHEDRAL
THE TOMB OF
THOMAS MILDMAY
2005** C73707

A complete rebuilding of Chelmsford's parish church of St Mary began in the first half of the 15th century. The nave and clerestory were added in 1489 and the final details – the chancel, tower and south porch – were added in the early 1500s. A host of human-sized wooden angels hung from the nave's roof. Outside, the handsome new church was topped-off with an inscription requesting prayers 'for the good estat of the Townshyp of Chelmsford'. During the mid 17th century Chelmsford became a hotbed of religious extremism, with anti-idolatrous feelings running high. The pictures of Christ and the Virgin Mary were removed from the east window of St Mary's Church and what remained of the coloured glass – largely the shields of families who had helped to build the church – was smashed by a mob on Guy Fawkes night in 1641 (5th November). A few months later, the church's wooden angels were taken down from its roof and burned in the street.

Chelmsford's rebuilt 15th-century parish church of St Mary caved in on the evening of 17th January 1800. Earlier in the day, some workmen had been opening a vault between two columns in the 15th-century south arcade. This weakened the arcading sufficiently for it to fall down, bringing the roof with it, as well as the old inscription about the 'Townshyp of Chelmsford'. John Johnson, the County Surveyor, made a start on a church restoration scheme that kept local artisans busy for the next three years. Some of the rubble was dusted down and reused; other chunks were used to stop up potholes or to make new pavements for the High Street. Services were held in the Shire Hall until the restored St Mary's opened in 1803. Also in 1800, shortly after the roof of St Mary's Church at Chelmsford collapsed, the tower of All Saints' Church at Writtle, a mile west of Chelmsford, followed suit. The events prompted a local rhyme:

> 'Chelmsford church and Writtle steeple
> Both fell down, but killed no people.'

Did You Know?
CHELMSFORD
A MISCELLANY

St Mary's Church in Chelmsford is seen here in 1892, when it was merely the town's parish church – in 1914 it achieved new status as a cathedral at the hub of England's largest diocese. Prior to that, Chelmsford had at various times been within the dioceses of St Albans, Rochester or London. When the church became Chelmsford Cathedral its original dedication to St Mary was expanded to St Mary the Virgin, St Peter and St Cedd – the latter being a Northumbrian monk who came to Essex in the mid seventh century to bring Christianity to the pagan East Saxons. When Chelmsford became the centre of the new diocese, it pipped several other Essex applicants at the post – Barking, Colchester, Thaxted, Woodford, Waltham Abbey and West Ham were all disappointed.

CHELMSFORD, ST MARY'S PARISH CHURCH (NOW CHELMSFORD CATHEDRAL) 1892 31510

Chelmsford Cathedral is a welcome pocket of tranquility in a busy town centre, and a fascinating port-of-call for those interested in the town's history. The tombs of Thomas and Benjamin Mildmay sit comfortably alongside the cathedral's more modern fittings. Tattered regimental flags hang from the rafters of a building that is also alive with colourful modern textiles. A particular feature of the interior is the magnificent nave ceiling, made of plaster and coloured in pastel shades, which dates from John Johnson's restoration of the building in 1800-1803. An unusual modern feature on the south-eastern corner of the exterior of the cathedral is a carved figure of St Peter dressed in the clothes of a modern-day Essex fisherman, including a wool hat and waders, and carrying the Key of Heaven in the form of a Yale key (photograph C73717, opposite). Also of interest on the exterior are 16 stone carvings at the foot of the battlements, representing the history of Chelmsford and the cathedral building, and the weathervane, which depicts a dragon emerging from the sun.

CHELMSFORD, THE CATHEDRAL, THE INTERIOR 1919 69024

CHELMSFORD, THE CATHEDRAL THE ST PETER STATUE 2005
C73717

Did You Know?
CHELMSFORD
A MISCELLANY

The man who founded the Colony of Connecticut in the USA worked in Chelmsford for a few years. He was Thomas Hooker, and he was installed in St Mary's Church (now the Cathedral) in 1626 as a curate and the Town Lecturer – an additional preacher. He was a charismatic speaker, but Bishop Laud of London, in whose diocese Chelmsford then was, did not approve of his outspoken views and Puritan tendencies, and in 1629 Hooker was turfed out. He fled to Holland, and from there he emigrated to the Massachusetts Bay Colony in America. However, he fell out with Puritan leaders in Massachusetts and left the colony with a breakaway group to establish the town of Hartford in the Connecticut River valley, which led to the founding of the Connecticut Colony. Thomas Hooker's link with Chelmsford is remembered with the Hooker Memorial Civic Plaque in a narrow alleyway just outside the cathedral grounds, opposite the south porch. It reads:

> *'Thomas Hooker, 1586 - 1647, Curate at St. Mary's Church and Chelmsford Town Lecturer 1626-29. Founder of the State of Connecticut, Father of American Democracy.'*

Essex has the unhappy distinction of having executed more witches than any other county in England's history, and the first major trial in the country for witchcraft itself, as the main indictment, took place in Chelmsford in 1566 when 63-year-old Agnes Waterhouse of Hatfield Peverell was found guilty and hanged. A series of witch trials took place in Chelmsford in the 16th and 17th centuries, and a number of unfortunate women were found guilty and hanged, but the most notorious witch trials took place in 1645 during the reign of terror of the notorious Matthew Hopkins of Manningtree, the self-styled 'Witchfinder General'. One of the most unpleasant characters in the county's history, Matthew Hopkins claimed to hold the 'Devil's own list of all the witches in England', and many towns in East Anglia paid him to come and search for witches in their area. As a result of his initial investigations 29 women were accused of being witches and tried at the Chelmsford assizes in July 1645. 19 women were found guilty and were hanged, 4 at Manningtree and the remaining 15 at Chelmsford.

Did You Know?
CHELMSFORD
A MISCELLANY

King Edward VI Grammar School – known as KEGS – was theoretically founded by that monarch in 1551. In fact, he was simply presenting a new charter to a church school that had existed since the 14th century. The Grammar School has its roots in a 14th-century chapel that once stood in St Mary's churchyard. Sir John Mounteney had founded this as a chantry, providing money for a priest to sing commemorative masses there. By the early 16th century, the chantry priest was holding a school in the chapel. It was given the government's seal of approval in 1551, and this is regarded as the official date of the school's founding. The Broomfield Road premises pictured below in 1892, the year of their completion, were the school's third proper home. Before it decamped to Broomfield Road, the school had formerly stood in Duke Street – the entrance to the old buildings being just to the left of the Coach and Horses Inn on the right hand side of photograph 56883 on the following pages, where the tree is. Among the former pupils of the pre-1551 Grammar School was the famous scientist, mathematician and necromancer Dr John Dee, who became astrologer and adviser on scientific matters to Elizabeth I.

CHELMSFORD, THE GRAMMAR SCHOOL 1892 31516

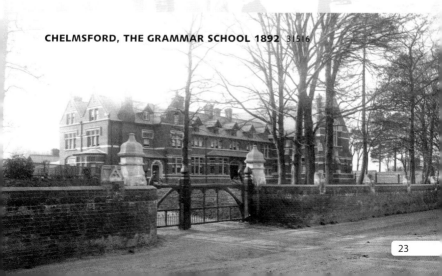

Did You Know?
CHELMSFORD
A MISCELLANY

During the medieval period the town expanded, spreading westwards along what was then called Brochole Street, but is now known as Duke Street. Duke Street was named after the Duk family, who owned land there in the 15th century.

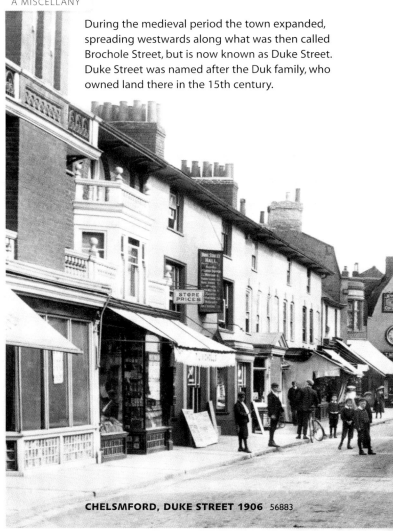

CHELMSFORD, DUKE STREET 1906 56883

Did You Know?
CHELMSFORD
A MISCELLANY

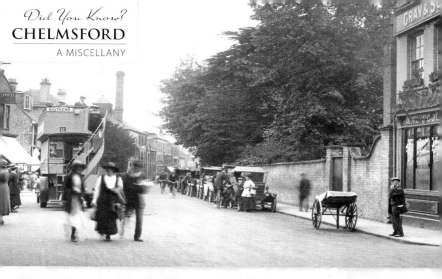

CHELMSFORD, DUKE STREET 1919 69017

The pub on the right hand side of photograph 69017 (above) is the Railway Tavern, now the Railway Arms. The tall chimney in the background belongs to Wells & Perry's Chelmsford Brewery, established in the 1780s. Chelmsford Brewery owned a number of local pubs. The photograph on the opposite page shows one of them, the Lion and Lamb (aka 'The Animals') in Duke Street in 1919, which backed right onto the Chelmsford Brewery. Statues of both creatures in the pub's name can be seen on the pediment at the top of the building. The Chelmsford Brewery works were demolished in 1936, and today there is a new pub building on the Lion & Lamb site.

In front of the Civic Centre in Duke Street is the Cenotaph, commemorating men from the Borough of Chelmsford who died in the First World War of 1914-18. However, the Cenotaph is only part of the memorial, for inside the Civic Centre, on the landing of the main staircase, is a series of four bronze panels inscribed with the names of nearly 400 local men who died in the conflict.

Did You Know?
CHELMSFORD
A MISCELLANY

**CHELMSFORD
DUKE STREET
THE LION & LAMB
1919** 69015v

Did You Know?
CHELMSFORD
A MISCELLANY

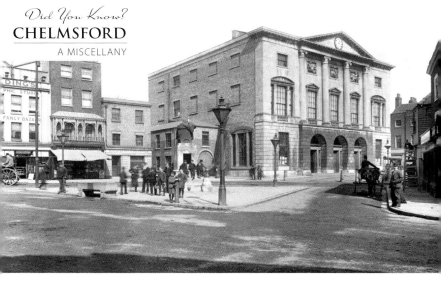

CHELMSFORD, THE SHIRE HALL 1892 31507

Chelmsford's most imposing public building is the Shire Hall that dominates Tindal Square, designed in 1789 by John Johnson, the County Surveyor. The foundation stone was laid alongside a box containing coins and metal tokens commemorating the passing of George III's latest bout of madness. The majestic new Shire Hall was finally ready in 1791. As well as courtrooms, it included cells, an armoury-room for the militia, and a room for storing market stalls. Many years ago the Shire Hall was where the Quarter Sessions trials were held, and prisoners were transferred there from the old police station at the corner of New Street and Waterloo Lane (the building with the spire in the photograph on the opposite page) via a tunnel under New Street. The old police station was sold off years ago, after the construction of the new police station at the traffic lights in New Street and Victoria Road, and the tunnel was bricked up halfway across for security reasons.

In front of the Shire Hall in the photograph below is the 36-pounder Russian cannon which was captured from Sebastopol during the Crimean War and presented to the town in 1858. It is seen here in its original position – it now stands in Oaklands Park, in front of the Essex Regiment Museum building. The building immediately behind the policeman in this view is the old Edwardian police station on the corner of New Street and Waterloo Lane on the site of the Greyhound Inn. In the 18th century Waterloo Lane was known as Greyhound Lane after the inn, and was also called Liver Lane at one time – the name derived from lévrier, the French word for greyhound.

An unusual attraction in Chelmsford is The Essex Police Museum, based at Essex Police Headquarters off Sandford Road at Springfield, which tells the story of law enforcement in Essex and the history of the county's police force since 1840. It holds a fascinating collection including a large photographic archive, as well as personnel, disciplinary and other records and documents and displays about some notorious cases. It is open on Wednesday afternoons and the first Saturday of each month from 10.30am – 4.30pm. It is free, and no appointment is needed.

CHELMSFORD
THE SHIRE HALL
1919 69021

Tindal Square and Tindal Street are named after one of Chelmsford's most famous sons, Sir Nicholas Conyngham Tindal (1776-1846), Chief Justice of Common Pleas, who was born in 1776 in Moulsham Street (near where Lloyds TSB Bank now is) and educated at the Grammar School. Judge Tindal was responsible for two significant legal rulings: one was the inception of the special verdict of 'Not Guilty by reason of insanity' at the trial of Daniel M'Naghten (known as 'the M'Naghten Rules'), and the other was in the case of Regina v Hale, when he ruled that where a defendant was provoked to such an unreasonable degree that he lost his self-control and killed the person responsible for that provocation, the defendant would be guilty of manslaughter, not murder. Tindal's reforms to the application of the criminal law, recognising the importance of differing states of mind (mens rea) with regard to vulnerable prisoners accused of serious crimes, were social reforms of great importance.

After Judge Tindal's death in 1846, his admirers – the Tindal Testimonial Committee – commissioned a statue of him from the sculptor H E Baily. It was erected in 1851, after much wrangling. The original idea had been to put it directly in front of the Shire Hall, but in the end it was placed over the site of the shut-off conduit-head in the market place (then called Conduit Square), when the conduit-head rotunda was moved to the junction of High Street and Springfield Road (as seen on page 15). Conduit Square and Conduit Street (or Back Street) were then renamed Tindal Square and Tindal Street. During the 20th century, the Tindal statue was unceremoniously shunted around the square in various road-widening schemes, in order to ease traffic-flow. In the photograph on the opposite page, taken c1965, the Judge sits in front of the vacant space left by the demolition of the Bell Inn.

**CHELMSFORD, JUDGE TINDAL STATUE
c1965** C73071

Did You Know?
CHELMSFORD
A MISCELLANY

One of the factors in Chelmsford's growth in the 19th century was the opening of the Chelmer & Blackwater Navigation in 1797, which enabled ships to reach the town. This involved the canalisation of the River Chelmer between Chelmsford and Maldon – in other words, the river was widened and deepened and, where necessary, given new, straight cuts. One of these cuts branched off the river just below Moulsham Mill and terminated in a basin off Springfield Road. In the pre-railway age, when most main roads were potential quagmires, canals were the best arteries of long-distance haulage. Rough plans for a canal had been mooted as early as the 1670s, but it was not until 1792 that the celebrated engineer John Rennie was called in. He made preliminary plans, and then mainly directed the work by post. The navvies completed the job in less than three years. For a few decades Chelmsford's canal basin was a buzz of commercial activity, with an array of private and public wharves around it. Not just coal, but chalk, meal, grain, flour and timber all passed through. The haulage of raw material offered by the canal was vital to Chelmsford's expansion, with an ongoing programme of development and rebuilding. One of the new buildings was the new gaol, built well away from the town at the top of Springfield Hill. The new gaol – a vast complex of seven radiating wings – opened in 1828.

Springfield, a parish of the Borough of Chelmsford north of the River Chelmer, started to grow after the canal-basin arrived there in the late 18th century. Before that, it was a peaceful, rural place centred around its green and All Saints' parish church, admired for its brick tower, which has a nave dating back to the 12th century. A former resident of Springfield, a William Pynchon, was one of the early American colonists, founding Springfield in Massachusetts. Born in Springfield in 1590, he sailed to New England in 1630 with the Winthrop Fleet. In 1636 he led a party of settlers to the Connecticut River, and began the settlement of Agawam, which he named Springfield after his home town in England.

Did You Know?
CHELMSFORD
A MISCELLANY

Victorian Chelmsford really began in 1839. For more than 200 years, the town's expansion had been restricted by the constraints of the Mildmay Entail – the clause in the will of Thomas Mildmay (died 1566), Henry VIII's auditor, that specified keeping the Mildmay family estate in one piece (see page 17). In 1833, however, an Act was passed that offered a get-out clause, and the Mildmays jumped at the chance. Things got under way in 1839 when two large farms in Moulsham were auctioned off. (The Mildmay family eventually sold the last remnants of its Chelmsford property in 1917.) The vast majority of the land was bought by the Chelmsford Company, a syndicate of five local nonconformists, who set to develop it into what was effectively a new suburb. This development centred on a new London road that bypassed narrow, old-fashioned Moulsham Street and created an entry into the town more in keeping with modern sensibilities. The new road became New London Road – Moulsham Street being the 'old' London Road. The new road crossed the Can by means of an Iron Bridge designed by a young local architect called James Fenton. In contrast to the Stone Bridge built by John Johnson, the Iron Bridge was a piece of functional design that was completed in 1840. After crossing the bridge, the new road headed east to join Conduit Street.

In 1888 the Iron Bridge was wrenched away by a flood that left Moulsham Street and Friars Place several feet deep in water. The flood was the latest in a series that had dogged the town during the 19th century. Back in 1824, the engineer Thomas Telford had been brought in to investigate the problem. No mean bridge-builder himself, he put it down to John Johnson's Stone Bridge with its worryingly pinched span. He had recommended dismantling it but this, of course, was not done, and the threat of flooding remained. A new Iron Bridge was constructed in 1890 to replace James Fenton's ill-fated construction, which is seen next to the Congregational Church in photograph 35524 on page 34.

CHELMSFORD, THE CONGREGATIONAL CHURCH 1895 35524

The handsome Congregational Church seen in photograph 35524 (above) was built on the New London Road beside the Iron Bridge over the Can in 1840, also designed by the local architect James Fenton. When finished, it was one of the largest chapels in the country, with seats for up to 2,000 worshippers. Since the owners of the Chelmsford Brewery were among the prime movers in the New London Road project, the chapel was given a pulpit in the shape of a beer-keg to acknowledge their contribution. By the time of the New London Road Congregational Church's demolition in 1971, its congregation had amalgamated with that of Baddow Road Congregational Church and built the new Christ Church on the site of a former brickyard in New London Road. The former site of the Congregational Church is currently (2011) occupied by the Dansk furniture store. However, another building by James Fenton that still stands today is the Mechanics' Institute, built in 1841 on the other side of the road opposite the Congregational Church to accommodate the activities of the Chelmsford Literary Society.

By 1842, houses were appearing in New London Road. James Fenton lived in one himself, and it is grimly ironic that the first burial in the new cemetery that opened on New London Road in 1846 was of his teenage son – Fenton was one of the trustees who contributed funds towards the establishment of the cemetery. One of the graves in the cemetery is of a man who had been a slave in New Orleans; he escaped and somehow ended up in Chelmsford, where he worked at the London Road Iron Works. He died in 1875, and the inscription on his tombstone records the name he gave himself in his new life – Joseph Freeman, 'who escaped to England and became also a Free Man in Christ'.

The photograph below shows the Infirmary & Dispensary on New London Road, built in 1883. The Infirmary – later known as London Road Hospital, and then as Chelmsford & Essex Hospital – closed its wards and most departments in the 1980s, although the centre part was retained for a small range of services for a time. Its frontage still stands, and is a protected building. To its right is the Ebenezer Strict Baptist Chapel. This view has now changed almost beyond recognition.

**CHELMSFORD
NEW LONDON ROAD AND THE INFIRMARY
1892** 31514

Did You Know?
CHELMSFORD
A MISCELLANY

Even before the Mildmay Entail was broken in 1839, Dame Jane Mildmay had sold a couple of fields to the Eastern Counties Railway. There were plans to push a new line from Bishopsgate in London to Colchester – and Chelmsford lay on the route. The railway line was opened when it got as far as Colchester, and the first passenger train passed through Chelmsford on 29th March 1843. Chelmsford's low-lying site necessitated the construction of three major viaducts for the railway line – a total of 83 arches in all – and an army of bricklayers had to be drafted in. The viaduct seen in the background of this view of the lake in Central Park was completed in 1842 and consists of 18 arches. It took shape at an incredible rate of 80,600 bricks per day. Central Park (formerly known as 'the Rec') opened in 1894. The lake in the park was first created in the 1840s, being the pit that was left after sufficient earth had been dug to make the railway embankment. The Borough Council leased the lake in 'the Rec' from the railway company for use as a bathing pond – although it was made somewhat redundant in 1906, when an outdoor swimming pool was opened in Waterloo Lane.

**CHELMSFORD, THE CAN VIADUCT
1895** 35518

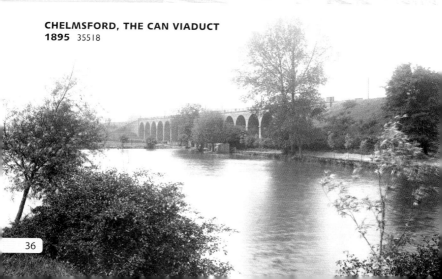

CHELMSFORD, HIGH STREET 1898 41504

This is another view of the old conduit-head rotunda when it stood at the junction of Springfield Road and High Street, this time looking towards Shire Hall. To the right of this view, the premises of Barnard, Cabinet Maker, Upholsterer and Decorator and also the Barnards Hotel occupies the former site of the Black Boy Inn, Chelmsford's once-famous coaching inn – its coaching trade was killed off by the advent of the railway in the 1840s, and the inn was demolished in 1857. As a young newspaper reporter, the future author Charles Dickens stayed at the Black Boy one wet weekend in January 1835 when he was sent to Chelmsford to cover the election there for the 'Morning Chronicle', and had a miserable time – although he did later mention the inn in a passing reference in 'The Pickwick Papers'. Dickens described Chelmsford as 'the dullest and most stupid place on earth' with nothing to look at in the town except for 'two immense prisons large enough to hold all the inhabitants of the county'. His main complaint though was that Chelmsford had no Sunday newspapers!

Industry came to Chelmsford in the 19th century, with a number of important companies in the town's story setting up in business here.

A millwright called John Bewley established the town's first iron-foundry in New Street in 1808. His son set up a new foundry in Anchor Street, and after the Bewleys faded out of the picture the Anchor Street Ironworks were taken over by T H P Dennis, and production began to focus on steam- and water-valves. A new partner and authority on electrical engineering, Colonel Rookes Evelyn Bell Crompton, joined the firm in 1875 and transformed it into Crompton's Arc Electric Works. Now specializing in the forward-looking field of electric lighting, Crompton's Arc Works moved to a much larger site on Writtle Road after their Anchor Street premises burned down in 1895. The firm were pioneers of electric lighting – they illuminated Crystal Palace and the Vienna Opera House, among other places – but made other machinery too, such as some of the early tube trains. In 1927 the firm merged with a Yorkshire company and, now trading as Crompton Parkinson, became one of the Chelmsford's biggest employers until the company was downsized and moved elsewhere in 1969. A housing development called 'The Village' now covers the factory site, but the company is recalled in the name of some of the roads, such as Rookes Crescent, Crompton Street and Evelyn Drive, and the impressive frontage of the Arc Works remains along Writtle Road.

In 1894, an engineer called Thomas Clarkson invented a steam car. Running off a paraffin-fired boiler, it could attain speeds of up to 20mph. Clarkson took over Colonel Crompton's old Anchor Street premises in 1902. The following year he produced his first steam omnibuses, and began supplying them to London's transport operators, who until then had relied on horse-drawn services. In 1909 he formed the National Steam Bus Company, which later became the National Omnibus Company. In 1918 they built the town's bus station on a site facing onto Duke Street, which was reconstructed and extended in the 1930s as a fine piece of functional art deco architecture (see photograph C73045x, opposite page). The building was demolished in 2005, and a new bus terminal in Duke Street opened in 2007.

Another important name in Chelmsford's story was the firm of Hoffmann's, which was formally established in 1898. Its factory stood at the corner of Rectory Lane and New Street, now recalled in the name of Hoffmanns Way. In the 1890s, two cousins called Geoffrey and Charles Barrett had started a factory making ball-bearings for bicycles, but had difficulty making the bearings round – which was a fairly fundamental requirement. They called upon the services of Ernst Hoffmann, a well-known expert in the field, and by 1901 they were properly up and running. At first, they only made bearings for bicycles, but were soon catering for the automobile market too. Hoffmann's were great survivors; they went with the flow of technological advancement, producing bearings for cars, aeroplanes and any other machinery that was developed. The firm spent its later decades in Chelmsford as Ransom, Hoffmann, Pollard (RHP), but the factory was closed in 1989 and most of it was demolished in 1990. The site is now occupied by the Rivermead Campus of the Anglia Ruskin University.

CHELMSFORD, THE BUS STATION c1955 C73045x

Did You Know?
CHELMSFORD
A MISCELLANY

The most famous industrial name in Chelmsford's story is probably that of the Marconi company. Guglielmo Marcono arrived in Chelmsford in 1898, at the age of 22. He was fascinated by electromagnetic waves, especially as a means of communication. Nobody in his native Italy, however, was prepared to support his ideas, and his Irish mother persuaded him to come to Britain. In 1899 he set up the world's first radio factory in a disused silk mill in Hall Street. The Essex landscape probably suited his purpose, as it had no hills to obstruct his waves. He took over John Hall's disused silk-factory in Hall Street and turned it into the Wireless, Telegraph and Signal Company Ltd. Much of his early work concentrated on aircraft radio. Within a decade, however, he had established radio links with continental Europe and the United States, and had scooped up a Nobel Prize for Physics. By 1912 the Hall Street site was proving too small, and a new works was built on the old cricket field in New Street, seen in photograph 69027 on page 41, opposite the goods yard and cattle pens belonging to the railway.

GUGLIELMO MARCONI F6133

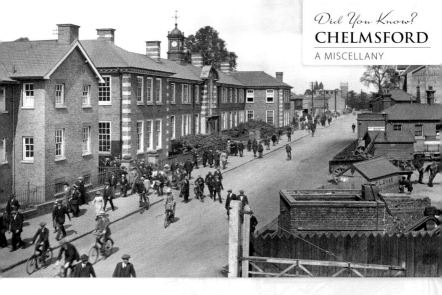

CHELMSFORD, NEW STREET, THE MARCONI WORKS 1920 69027

Marconi's New Street factory was the first purpose-built radio works in the world, and Britain's first publicised broadcast of entertainment was transmitted from there in 1920. This was a performance by the Australian soprano Dame Nellie Melba, who sang into a microphone cobbled together from a telephone receiver and a cigar box; this item is preserved in the Marconi collection of the Museum of the History of Science at Oxford. Capitalising on the success of this performance, the Marconi company set up a regular radio station in an ex-army hut at Writtle, just off Lawford Lane. The hut – known by its call sign, Two Emma Toc – is preserved with replica equipment in the industrial heritage centre at Sandford Mill, near Sandon; its original site is now a housing development called Melba Court. In the opening years of the 21st century, Marconi's (by then part of Marconi-Selenia Communications, and later Selex Communications) announced a scaling-down of its Chelmsford activities. The New Street factory was closed in 2008 and the company's remaining operations were moved to Basildon, ending more than 100 years of the Marconi connection with Chelmsford. The historic Marconi factory is currently (2011) empty and facing an uncertain future.

Did You Know?
CHELMSFORD
A MISCELLANY

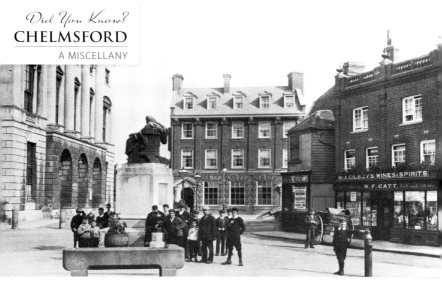

CHELMSFORD, TINDAL SQUARE 1906 56881

By the 1880s, Chelmsford was the only county town in England other than Oakham in Rutland that was not a borough – it had no charter, no council and no mayor. The application for borough status was eventually seen through by a Duke Street solicitor named Arthur Furbank. The charter that entitled the town to a system of self-government was sealed in London on 7th September 1888, and 12 days later Furbank triumphantly bore it into town. Contemporary photographs of the event show that this was a very big deal for Chelmsford – a sea of people filled every inch of Tindal Square to hear the terms of the charter declaimed from a platform. For most of the day an enormous procession of schoolchildren, firemen and Essex dignitaries snaked its way through the town. That night the town was illuminated by the electric lighting laid on by Crompton's Arc Works. This was only a temporary extravagance – the Council reverted to the cheaper option of gas lighting once the festivities were over – but Chelmsford, on top of everything else, had just become the first place in Britain to use electric streetlights.

Did You Know?
CHELMSFORD
A MISCELLANY

Probably one of the worst planning crimes in the town's history was the demolition of Tindal Street in 1969-71. It contained many timber-framed and Georgian buildings and also the Corn Exchange, the balustraded building at the end of the left-hand side of the street in the photograph below, on the corner with Tindal Square; this purpose-built structure opened for business in 1857, and it was here that local farmers came on Market Day to sell their produce to the corn merchants, who had stands on its trading floor. The Italianate façade of the grand building masked a long, glass-roofed trading area. After the decline of the agricultural industry the Corn Exchange entered a new role, as a dance hall, and during the 1960s this was where many famous artists appeared at the Saturday Scene. Sadly, the Corn Exchange was demolished in 1969. Over the next two years the whole west side of Tindal Street followed suit, to be replaced by the sidewall of High Chelmer, the new shopping precinct. It opened in 1972 and quickly earned Chelmsford a reputation as a place to come and shop – a reputation that the town still enjoys.

CHELMSFORD, TINDAL STREET 1919 69016

Fairs are a major part of Chelmsford's history. One of the town's strangest curios must be the area of Writtle Road cemetery reserved for the graves of travelling showmen. Displaying a robust attitude to the afterlife, the graves are adorned with gilded, marble pick-up trucks, or etched with representations of ferris-wheels and helter-skelters.

Chelmsford made a bid for city status to mark the new millennium in 2000. It has only ever been a city in ecclesiastical terms (ie it has a cathedral) and in the name of its football team. The bid was unsuccessful, but Chelmsford is applying for city status again in 2012, as part of Queen Elizabeth II's Diamond Jubilee celebrations. If the application is successful, Chelmsford will become Essex's first city.

Chelmsford has a number of well-organised festivals in its annual calendar. Both Moulsham Street and the town centre fill up with entertainers each year when the Christmas lights are turned on, and the cathedral hosts ten days of music and drama every spring. The Essex Poetry Festival comes to town in October, and in March the library hosts talks and readings from a range of well-known authors as part of the Essex Book Festival. In addition to the V Festival, Hylands Park also hosts the annual Chelmsford Spectacular, when names from the world of show business entertain weekend crowds of up to 30,000 people. There is also the Fling, a tented festival in the summer offering a variety of eclectic entertainments and amusements for adults, whilst younger Chelmsfordians have their own annual event of activities and fun – the 3 foot People Festival, the only festival in the UK held specifically for under five-year-olds.

Imagine what William de Sainte-Mère-Église – the 12th-century Bishop of London who founded Chelmsford market – would think if he were to visit the town today. He would have trouble recognising the place. But it would be nice to think that, having got over his surprise, he would be delighted: 800-odd years down the line, his new town is still a thriving centre of commercial and cultural activity.

Did You Know?
CHELMSFORD
A MISCELLANY

CHELMSFORD, THE MEADOWS 2005 C73723

SPORTING CHELMSFORD

Amongst Chelmsford's earliest sporting fixtures were the Chelmsford Races on Galleywood Common, commemorated in Galleywood's colourful village sign. The races were a great social occasion locally. They took place from at least 1759 until 1935, but were probably held even earlier. The hilly nature of the course made it demanding of both horse and rider. After flat racing gave way to steeplechasing in 1892, the course offered jockeys the unique opportunity to steeplechase round an actual steeple – that of Galleywood's church, the only church in the country to be completely encircled by a racecourse. In the 18th century the race meeting was a three day event with races for a plate of £50 each. The horses for each day's plate had to be entered into the races at the Black Boy Inn in Chelmsford on the Saturday before the race meeting.

A Chelmsford Cricket Club was formed in 1811, initially playing on a field in New Street. From the 1920s the club rented a riverside meadow from the Wenley family; this was later adopted by the County club, which is still based there, whilst Chelmsford Cricket Club is now based at Chelmer Park. The present-day Essex County Cricket Club plays most of its home games at the Ford County Ground in New Writtle Street in Chelmsford, but also plays at Lower Castle Park in Colchester and Garons Park at Southend. A great name in Essex Cricket Club's history is Graham Gooch, OBE, DL (born 1953), who played for the county between 1973 and 1997, and captained both Essex and England. A statue of Graham Gooch stands beside a pathway off New London Road just past the old Infirmary frontage, close to the County Cricket Ground in New Writtle Street.

The Chelmsford Rugby Football Club was established in 1920 and currently (2011) plays in London Division North East 2 division. The club is based at Coronation Park on Timpsons Lane.

The earliest reference to football being played in Chelmsford dates from 1394, when 11 respectable Townsmen of Chelmsford were hauled before the manor-court for 'playing at ball…over the church'. Chelmsford's football club dates from more recent times, being originally founded as Chelmsford FC in 1878. At first the club shared the cricket club's New Street pitch, but eventually found its own home at New Writtle Street, on a field that appears to be where Moulsham once buried its plague victims. The club folded in 1938 but was refounded as Chelmsford City FC that same year and entered the Southern League. The club, nicknamed 'The Clarets', won the Southern League title in 1946, 1968 and 1972. A more recent triumph was in 2008 with the club winning the Isthmian League Premier Division title, earning promotion to the Conference South (currently – 2011 – known as Blue Square Bet South). Chelmsford City FC is now based at Chelmsford Sports & Athletics Centre in Salerno Way, which is also the home of Chelmsford Athletics Club.

Chelmsford Hockey Club is one of the most successful hockey clubs in the country with a thriving membership at its base in Chelmer Park. The Ladies' 1st XI competes in the English Hockey League Premier Division and the Men's 1st XI competes in the English Hockey League Division 1.

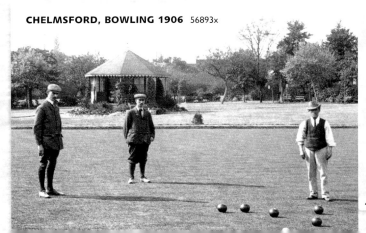

CHELMSFORD, BOWLING 1906 56893x

QUIZ QUESTIONS

Answers on page 52.

1. Whereabouts in Chelmsford can you find Justice, Wisdom and Mercy?

2. What is the motto on the coat of arms of Chelmsford Borough Council?

3. In the 1980s, Chelmsford was the location of a TV sitcom series – what was it?

4. Why is Admiral's Park so named?

5. Which punk band performed at Chelmsford Gaol in 1976?

6. What sport is played by the Chelmsford Chieftains?

7. What is 'The Naiad', and whereabouts in Chelmsford can you find it?

8. What is known as 'The Chelmsford Sissies' and where can you find it?

9. Which famous drinks company that is still a major employer in the Chelmsford area started in a chemist's shop in Tindal Street?

10. With which European towns is Chelmsford twinned?

CHELMSFORD, TINDAL STREET 1919 56882

RECIPE

CHELMSFORD PUDDING

This pudding is made with a sponge topping over a layer of stewed fruit. This version uses apples, but the same amount of any other stewed fruit of choice can be used.

>   225g/8oz prepared weight of cooking apples,
>   peeled, cored and sliced
>   75ml/3fl oz water
>   50g/2oz butter or margarine,
>   softened to room temperature
>   50g/2oz caster sugar
>   1 egg
>   150ml/5fl oz/ ¼ pint milk
>   115g/4oz self-raising flour
>   A pinch of salt
>   A little extra caster sugar for sprinkling
>   on top of the baked pudding

Put the sliced apples into a saucepan with the water. Bring to the boil, then cover the pan and reduce the heat to low. Simmer very gently for about 15-20 minutes, until the apples are soft, then remove from the heat.

Pre-heat the oven to 180°C/350°F/Gas Mark 4. Grease a 1.2 litres (2 pint) pie dish.

Beat together the butter or margarine and sugar until light and fluffy. Beat together the egg and the milk, then gradually add it into the mixture, alternating with the sifted flour and salt. Beat it all together well to make a smooth mixture. Put the stewed fruit and any remaining liquid in a layer in the pie dish. Pour the sponge mixture over and make sure that it is spread to the edges, to cover the fruit. Bake in the pre-heated oven for 30-40 minutes, until the topping is risen and golden, and firm to the touch. Remove from the oven and sprinkle some extra sugar over the top whilst it is still hot. Serve with cream, custard or ice-cream.

Did You Know?
CHELMSFORD
A MISCELLANY

RECIPE

SEED CAKE

For many centuries, local farmers came to Chelmsford to trade their grain with the corn merchants. In his 'Five Hundred Points of Good Husbandry', the Essex farmer, poet and author Thomas Tusser (1524–1580) referred to the East Anglian custom of serving Seed Cake (flavoured with caraway seeds) to farm-workers when the wheat-sowing was completed:

> 'Wife, some time this weeke, if the wether hold clear
> And end of wheat-sowing we make for this yeare.
> Remember you, therefore, though I do it not.
> The Seed-cake, the pasties and Furmentie-pot.'

The seed cake that Mrs Tusser made in the 16th century would have been an enriched bread dough. This 19th-century version results in a sponge cake flavoured with caraway seeds, commonly used in British cookery in the past to give a slightly aniseedy flavour to cakes, breads, buns and biscuits.

    175g/6oz butter
    175g/6oz caster sugar
    3 eggs, beaten
    2 teaspoonfuls of caraway seeds
    225g/8oz plain flour
    1 teaspoonful baking powder
    1 tablespoonful ground almonds
    A pinch of salt
    1 tablespoonful milk

Pre-heat the oven to 180°C/350°F/Gas Mark 4 (slightly less for a fan oven). Grease and line an 18cm (7 inch) cake tin. Cream together the butter and sugar until light and fluffy. Gradually add in the beaten eggs, a little at a time, adding a little flour if necessary to prevent the mixture curdling. Mix in the caraway seeds. Sift the flour, salt and baking powder together and use a large metal spoon to fold it into the mixture. Add the ground almonds and then the milk, to form a soft dropping consistency. Pour the mixture into the prepared tin and level the surface. Bake in the pre-heated oven for about one hour, until the sponge is risen and golden and firm to the touch. Leave in the tin for 5 minutes before turning out onto a wire tray to cool.

QUIZ ANSWERS

1. The three panels beneath the pediment on the front of the Shire Hall represent Wisdom, Mercy and Justice (seen in photograph 69021 on page 29). The County Assizes were held in the Shire Hall for almost 200 years, until the main crown court complex for Essex was opened in 1982 in New Street, and these panels were reminders of the qualities to be borne in mind by the judges and juries who sat in the building.

2. The motto on the current armorial bearings of Chelmsford Borough Council, that were granted on 3rd March, 1975, is 'Many Minds, One Heart'.

3. In 1988, 'Caesaromagus', the name of the Roman town at Chelmsford, became the improbable setting for a BBC sitcom. 'Chelmsford 123' was a comedy series set in the Roman town in the year AD123. The show concerned the attempts of the ineffectual Roman governor Aulus Paulinus to subdue Badvoc, the unruly leader of the local British tribesmen. The main characters – both wholly fictitious – were respectively played by Jimmy Mulville and Rory McGrath, who also wrote the series. It ran for two seasons.

4. Admiral's Park was named after John Faithful Fortescue, a rear-admiral who died in 1820, who once owned Writtle Lodge near the footbridge on the River Can, close to the pitch and putt course in the adjoining West Park.

5. The Sex Pistols performed at Chelmsford Gaol on 17th September 1976. They apparently managed to win over their captive audience, though stories that John Lydon tried to instigate a prison riot have been greatly exaggerated. In 1990 a recording of the concert was released, titled 'Live at Chelmsford Top Security Prison'.

6. The Chelmsford Chieftains are an ice-hockey team, based at the Riverside Ice and Leisure Centre, the only ice skating rink in Essex. They play in the English National Ice Hockey League.

7. The Naiad is the stone water nymph that stands in the foyer of the Shire Hall. She was made in 1791 as a decoration for the conduit-head of the water supply in what is now Tindal Square, as a six-foot water nymph grasping a shield and standing on a podium encircled by writhing dolphins. Her tenure there did not last long: there were problems with the conduit's water flow, and in 1812 the Naiad was removed and replaced by the rotunda, the domed, circular edifice that now stands in Tower Gardens (see photograph C73032, page 15). The Naiad then spent 150 years as a garden ornament in Springfield, gradually losing parts of her body. In the early 1960s she was given to the Borough Council and placed in the foyer of the Shire Hall.

8. It is not every year that a Chelmsford artist wins the Turner Prize for Art – but Grayson Perry did just that in 2003. He was educated at KEGS and then took an art foundation course at Braintree College. Perry's challenging ceramics include the pot called 'The Chelmsford Sissies', which he has presented to Chelmsford Museum. It depicts a fictional transvestite festival in Chelmsford, but Perry's inspiration for 'The Chelmsford Sissies' was a true story from the time of the Civil War, when the Royalist Sir Thomas Sissye surrendered his men to Parliamentary forces. As an act of humiliation, Sir Thomas and his men were forced to parade through Chelmsford wearing women's dresses.

9. The soft drink company Britvic – previously the British Vitamin Company – originated in Chelmsford in Victorian times, when a chemist in Tindal Street experimented with fruit-flavoured waters. Britvic moved to its present home, at Widford, in the 1950s, where its monolithic clock tower is one of Chelmsford's landmarks, at 100ft (30.5 metres) high.

10. Chelmsford's twin towns are Backnang in Germany and Annonay in France – which is also twinned with Backnang. Chelmsford also has links with Chelmsford in the USA, in the state of Massachusetts, although it is not officially twinned with it. Between the Meadows and the River Chelmer is Backnang Square, which commemorates Chelsmford's German twin town with a piece of modern art, the Backnang Friendship Sculpture.

FRANCIS FRITH

PIONEER VICTORIAN PHOTOGRAPHER

Francis Frith, founder of the world-famous photographic archive, was a complex and multi-talented man. A devout Quaker and a highly successful Victorian businessman, he was philosophical by nature and pioneering in outlook. By 1855 he had already established a wholesale grocery business in Liverpool, and sold it for the astonishing sum of £200,000, which is the equivalent today of over £15,000,000. Now in his thirties, and captivated by the new science of photography, Frith set out on a series of pioneering journeys up the Nile and to the Near East.

INTRIGUE AND EXPLORATION

He was the first photographer to venture beyond the sixth cataract of the Nile. Africa was still the mysterious 'Dark Continent', and Stanley and Livingstone's historic meeting was a decade into the future. The conditions for picture taking confound belief. He laboured for hours in his wicker dark-room in the sweltering heat of the desert, while the volatile chemicals fizzed dangerously in their trays. Back in London he exhibited his photographs and was 'rapturously cheered' by members of the Royal Society. His reputation as a photographer was made overnight.

VENTURE OF A LIFE-TIME

By the 1870s the railways had threaded their way across the country, and Bank Holidays and half-day Saturdays had been made obligatory by Act of Parliament. All of a sudden the working man and his family were able to enjoy days out, take holidays, and see a little more of the world.

With typical business acumen, Francis Frith foresaw that these new tourists would enjoy having souvenirs to commemorate their days out. For the next thirty years he travelled the country by train and by pony and trap, producing fine photographs of seaside resorts and beauty spots that were keenly bought by millions of Victorians. These prints were painstakingly pasted into family albums and pored over during the dark nights of winter, rekindling precious memories of summer excursions. Frith's studio was soon supplying retail shops all over the country, and by 1890 F Frith & Co had become the greatest specialist photographic publishing company in the world, with over 2,000 sales outlets, and pioneered the picture postcard.

FRANCIS FRITH'S LEGACY

Francis Frith had died in 1898 at his villa in Cannes, his great project still growing. By 1970 the archive he created contained over a third of a million pictures showing 7,000 British towns and villages.

Frith's legacy to us today is of immense significance and value, for the magnificent archive of evocative photographs he created provides a unique record of change in the cities, towns and villages throughout Britain over a century and more. Frith and his fellow studio photographers revisited locations many times down the years to update their views, compiling for us an enthralling and colourful pageant of British life and character.

We are fortunate that Frith was dedicated to recording the minutiae of everyday life. For it is this sheer wealth of visual data, the painstaking chronicle of changes in dress, transport, street layouts, buildings, housing and landscape that captivates us so much today, offering us a powerful link with the past and with the lives of our ancestors.

Computers have now made it possible for Frith's many thousands of images to be accessed almost instantly. The archive offers every one of us an opportunity to examine the places where we and our families have lived and worked down the years. Its images, depicting our shared past, are now bringing pleasure and enlightenment to millions around the world a century and more after his death.

For further information visit: www.francisfrith.com

INTERIOR DECORATION

Frith's photographs can be seen framed and as giant wall murals in thousands of pubs, restaurants, hotels, banks, retail stores and other public buildings throughout Britain. These provide interesting and attractive décor, generating strong local interest and acting as a powerful reminder of gentler days in our increasingly busy and frenetic world.

FRITH PRODUCTS

All Frith photographs are available as prints and posters in a variety of different sizes and styles. In the UK we also offer a range of other gift and stationery products illustrated with Frith photographs, although many of these are not available for delivery outside the UK – see our web site for more information on the products available for delivery in your country.

THE INTERNET

Over 100,000 photographs of Britain can be viewed and purchased on the Frith web site. The web site also includes memories and reminiscences contributed by our customers, who have personal knowledge of localities and of the people and properties depicted in Frith photographs. If you wish to learn more about a specific town or village you may find these reminiscences fascinating to browse. Why not add your own comments if you think they would be of interest to others? See **www.francisfrith.com**

PLEASE HELP US BRING FRITH'S PHOTOGRAPHS TO LIFE

Our authors do their best to recount the history of the places they write about. They give insights into how particular towns and villages developed, they describe the architecture of streets and buildings, and they discuss the lives of famous people who lived there. But however knowledgeable our authors are, the story they tell is necessarily incomplete.